SMALL TOWN
BIG CITY

haiku & senryu

Donald McLeod

STONE BUDDHA BOOKS

In memory of my parents,
who encouraged me
to have an artistic life.

ACKNOWLEDGEMENT

Most of the haiku in this collection originally appeared in the following publications: Frogpond, Modern Haiku, Wind Chimes, Brussels Sprout, Oak Grove Haiku, old pond, Inkstone, Dragonfly, Haiku Zasshi Zo, The Red Pagoda, New Cicada, Spoke (England), Vol. No. Magazine, The Archer, Parnassus, Slipstream, Kindred Spirit and Daybreak.

SMALL TOWN
BIG CITY

SMALL TOWN

small town ...
spitting into the same crack
again   and   again

winter afternoon ...
losing count of the cars
on a passing train

cold winter night –
the cat rubbing words
into my leg

old photo curling
on the dresser
grandfather touches his toes

in the attic –
a nest of mice
in my father's old hat

SunBurst Tavern . . .
old timers yellowing
with the wallpaper

old slippers
spilling comfort
by the brass bed

father's old watch
filling with rust
at ten after four

spring shower –
tadpoles diving
in the dented hubcap

pick-up window –
rented prom tux
flapping with excitement

a flock of starlings
reflected in the cow's
moist eye

spring buds
softening
the old walnut tree

the arc of your hand
scattering seeds
to the chickens

rooster
viewing each moment
from a new angle

cow's tongue
filling
the salt lick groove

after the shower –
croaking hoof prints
flashing in moonlight

old wooden wagon
its wheels rusted
into a right turn

half-buried tennis shoe
worn smooth
by the sea

fisherman's lined face
smiling through
the torn net

child
spits in the ocean
and runs

moonlit surf fish
flipping out
in tide shine

grandpa's old porch
paper milk stopper sunk deep
in the empty bottle

cripple man dozing . . .
his gnarled hand still gripping
the absent cane

after the funeral –
dressed up children
chasing a crow

foggy winter dawn –
rime ice coats
the fiddle neck plant

white orchid
clipped
in a mason jar

late afternoon –
sunlight glinting through
the baby's drool

dark prairie night
a concert of fireflies
in the road

a field mouse
wild-eyed in the piano –
Rachmaninoff

kitten
watching a toadstool
filling with moonlight

baby robins –
all beak
and no worm

trainer's pipe flame
flickering
in the mare's eye

sprig of green –
logging camp redwood stump
starting all over

summer birds singing
swirling ball of golden gnats
in the sunset

blurry old photo –
my first trout
lost against my shirt

Greyhound bus trip . . .
a child's loose marble
rolling with the land

father's thick hands
fumbling
with the Christmas gift

wind
slapping torn tin
on the desert shack

peace sign
filling with rust
on the hippy bus

small town –
post mistress
reading a postcard

new entries (2016 Edition)

dusk . . .
the old horse fades
into the pasture

winter sunday –
the chill of the back row
church pew

small town parade –
the mayor's prancing horse
passing wind

small town –
the hippy's haircut
talk of the feed store

small town –
the cheerleader's secret
starting to show

BIG CITY

bright city lights –
the moon
slips into a junkyard

L.A. stargazing –
half of them come down
and land

winter blizzard
courthouse bannister
ends in an icicle

Rockefeller Center –
tapered snow feathers
the bronze dove's wing

gray city day
a rustling of pigeons
in the gargoyle's mouth

chinese restaurant –
the waiter agreeing
with my question

chopsticks
adding flavor
to my rice kernel

chinatown shop –
the mexican man
tries on a kimono

lightning over the city –
war movie flickering
in the bedroom

a standing ovation
reflected in the blues singer's
dark glasses

B-movie set –
the rent-a-buffalo blinking
in a fake snowstorm

revival preacher
pointing
a jeweled finger

seagull
lands safely –
airport parking lot

bag lady's shadow
draining down
the park bench

America's Cup
victory parade –
homeless man waving

pigeon
decorating the war hero's
statue

paying taxes –
border trim remains
on the postage stamp

out of work –
checking the mailbox
on Sunday morning

TV cop show –
the escaping auto
hits a garbage can

short vacation
putting instant coffee
in the microwave

cocktail party
dentist peering
into his wife's purse

trade show psychic
        lost
  in the parking lot

fisherman's wharf –
seagull eying
a tourist's wrist watch

rear view mirror –
the lady who bumped me
does a mime show

half drunk
in a strange city –
bank machine gives me cash

metaphysical bookstore –
man in a toga
wearing bowling shoes

I exhale . . .
she rolls her fork
over the peas

damp tissues
in the pocket
of her winter coat

castle by the lake
turning the postcard
over and over

wanting her back . . .
parking tickets curling
on my windshield

divorce final –
stripper's phone number
blurred on a napkin

Beirut child
listening to the sea
in an artillery shell

Memorial Wall –
veteran's prosthetic hand
touching a comrade's name

war hero
oxidizing
on the gray building

homeless man
screaming
at the mannequin

security alert –
sparrow on the loose
in the shopping mall

slow afternoon . . .
hair stylist moussing
her baby's curl

puzzled child
rubbing the doll's
smooth crotch

construction worker
sharing his sandwich
with a sparrow

bag lady sitting
with bags – no
two bag ladies

old man
watching the merry-go-round ...
autumn chill

urban dog
intoxicated with scent
in the deep forest

dusk . . .
city snails stirring
in the plastic planter

New Entries (2016 Edition)

Hollywood Boulevard –
the Chicano boy spray paints
his star on the sidewalk

my Hollywood date
leaves a phone message
for her dog

street musician . . .
the emptiness of his
open guitar case

bad part of town –
the Virgin Mary yard statue
bolted to a pipe

summer heat . . .
slowing my step
at the wax museum

ABOUT THE AUTHOR

Donald McLeod was born in Edmonton, Alberta, Canada and grew up in Mendocino County in Northern California. He has written both fiction and non-fiction, screenplays, haiku and longer poetry. For five years he was co-editor of the literary journal *Vol. No. Magazine*. His poetry has been published in many literary magazines in North America, Europe and Japan.

McLeod has been a professional mime/movement artist for the past 46 years. He is perhaps best known for his work as the *American Tourister Gorilla* in the company's 15 year luggage campaign, and for his acting work in feature films, which include the gorilla in *Trading Places* & *The Man With Two Brains*, along with his portrayal of TC the werewolf, in the classic horror film *The Howling*. He lives in Los Angeles with his cat Benny, and a revolving collection of raccoons, possums, squirrels and wild birds.

www.zenbutoh.com
www.livingstatue.com
www.stonebuddhabooks.com

www.ingramcontent.com/pod-product-compliance
Lightning Source LLC
Chambersburg PA
CBHW020042040426
42331CB00030B/582